The Real Robinson Crusoe

What Should I Do?

MC PAQUIN

ISBN: 1927833531
ISBN-13: 9781927833537

CONTENTS

ACKNOWLEDGEMENT

(:   TERRY   :)

Note on the Format

After decades of devouring old letters, diaries, memoirs, speeches, and books by historians from long ago, MC Paquin, a teacher, created the "What Should I Do?" series of books to make history fun for her students.

The people are real, as are the incidents. The recounting is in the first person and conversations are taken from recorded words when possible; but when these were lacking, words and situations were added sparingly to impart the flavor of the actual actions taken -- and to bring the past vividly to life.

1 Samuel de Champlain: Surrender or Bluff?

What would you do if you were the leader of a colony, and enemies wanted you to surrender your fort?

It's the summer of 1628. My name's Samuel de Champlain. I'm a French explorer. Twenty years ago, I left France with 28 men to set up a fur trading post in the area you call Quebec City, Canada. We trade with the local First Peoples for furs. *But what a job I've had setting up a colony!* The businessmen in France who finance us don't care whether we live or die; they just want their profits from the fur trade. Every year my colony faces starvation because of a lack of supplies from France.

This morning, as I'm inspecting our food supply in the storehouse, my brother-in-law, Eustache, joins me. "Samuel," he says, "we're in big trouble. We have only 5 barrels of mouldy biscuits and a small stash of peas and beans. That won't go far with 55 people to feed." I shake my head and say, "Our supply ship from France should have been here by now."

As Eustache and I leave the building, two of my men walk into our settlement. One of the men says, *"Samuel, we have terrible news!* France and England are at war, and the English are coming here to capture our fort. They've already taken over our fur trading post, and now they're at our farm. They're stealing what they can make use of and burning everything else." Shocked, I say, *"Good grief!* We'll have to act quickly. Let's get everyone together. We'll have to barricade the fort."

The following morning, as Eustache and I are rushing around to help barricade the fort, some traders deliver a letter to me from David Kirke, the leader of the English. As I'm reading the letter, Eustache walks up to me. "Is the news very bad, Samuel?" he asks.

I nod. "Yes. Kirke says that he has captured our supply ship, stolen our food supplies, kidnapped the new colonists from France, and destroyed our buildings." I shake my head. "He's even issued me a threat, saying, 'Champlain, sooner or later, I'll get what I demand. For your sake, I wish to accomplish this by courteous means rather than force.'" I look up at Eustache. "Kirke says that he'll treat us well if we surrender the fort."

Eustache gives me a worried look. "Samuel, what will you do?"

TWO CHOICES FACE ME: I can surrender, or I can try to bluff the English.

What should I do?

Answer:

I decided to bluff the English. In a letter to Kirke, I lied about our bad situation. I said,

> "Kirke, we'll be able to defend our fort with the supplies we
> already have. You'll not find it easy to conquer us. My men are
> not short on courage. They've been through many difficult times in
> the past."

My bluff worked. The English went away. But during that winter, my colony suffered terribly from starvation.

When the English returned in the spring, we surrendered, and I was taken to England as a prisoner. Neither France nor England won the war, but peace was declared. The peace treaty gave France back her colonies in the New World.

Points of Interest:

To this day, the French in Canada think of Champlain as a hero for keeping a French colony in Canada when he had so little help from France. They call him the Father of New France.

The French had a different attitude from that of the English when they came to the land we now call Canada: while the French focused on fur trading and creating good relations with the First Peoples, the English concentrated on taking over the land.

France only showed an interest in settling Canada around 1663, when Louis XIV was King of France. King Louis sent over 1200 soldiers to stabilize the French-Iroquois situation, which had been hostile, and also encouraged 700 unmarried women to immigrate to New France by offering them money. This helped even out the men to women ratio, which had been 6:1. These women were called *filles du roi,* or daughters of the king.

There was little immigration from France after this. The 10,000 settlers reported on the 1681 census became the ancestors of almost all of today's French-speaking Canadians.

2 Alexander Mackenzie: Should We Fight, or Should We Try to Be Friends?

What would you do if you were an explorer in a new land, and you were threatened by some local people?

The year is 1793. My name's Alexander Mackenzie. I'm a 30-year-old explorer and a partner in a fur trading company based in Montreal in the country you call Canada.

These are exciting times. Explorers are racing to find river routes across North America. But exploring can be dangerous. There are many ways to die in this rugged land: you can drown while canoeing on rapids, freeze to death, starve, or die in fights with First Peoples who don't want you crossing their territory.

Not long ago, my company asked me to find a river route from the Rocky Mountains to the Pacific Ocean. They want to trade with the west coast First Peoples for furs. So far, no European has reached the west coast by land.

One month ago, I began my expedition from a fort on the east side of the Rockies. To help me, I brought nine men: Alexander Mackay, who is a fellow fur trader, two First Peoples who are guides, and six voyageurs. Voyageurs are tough men hired by fur trading companies to carry goods to and from remote areas.

Today is a warm June day. My men and I are high in the Rockies. For the past month the scenery has been beautiful, but our trip has been terrible. The mountain streams are often wild. Twice, our canoe smashed against rocks and had to be repaired. And the steep mountain canyons are nearly impossible to hike. My men are getting fed up.

At the moment, we're canoeing down a river. All of a sudden, we see two warriors standing on a riverbank. They're shaking their fists, waving their bows and arrows, and shouting at us. Their chests are bare, except for necklaces made of bear claws.

Mackay turns to me and says, *"Good grief, Alexander! We're in big trouble!"*

TWO CHOICES FACE ME: I can order my men to retreat, or I can try to make friends with the warriors.

What should I do?

Answer:

I commanded my men to paddle to the riverbank. Then I walked over to the warriors and shook their hands. They were very curious and looked us over thoroughly. It was the first time they'd seen white men. To our relief, they laid aside their weapons. One warrior, with a trembling hand, gave me his knife in a gesture of friendship. Luckily, the warriors let us continue on our journey.

Over the following weeks, we met several tribes. Some guided us towards the Pacific Ocean, which they called the "Stinking Lake".

One day, when some First Peoples saw us crash into rocks with our canoe, they sat down on the riverbank and cried, thinking we were done for.

Another tribe was so cheerful that I called their camp the Friendly Village. The men of this village dressed in fur robes. The old chief had a long beard, so I gave him a pair of scissors to clip his beard. He was overjoyed and used them right away.

My men and I finally made it to the Pacific Ocean. To mark the occasion, I mixed some red pigment with bear grease and painted a message on a huge rock we camped on overnight. I wrote,

> "Alexander Mackenzie, from Canada, by land, the twenty-second
> of July, one thousand seven hundred and ninety-three."

My men and I were the first Europeans to cross the Rockies and reach the Pacific Ocean by land.

Point of Interest:

If a spaceship landed near you and aliens got out and approached you, what would you do? Would you welcome them, attack them, or run like mad?

3 Charles Sturt: Danger on the Murray

What would you do if you were an explorer in a new territory, and you were threatened by hundreds of local people?

The year is 1830. My name's Charles Sturt. I'm a British explorer. At present, I'm exploring the greatest river in Australia: the Murray.

The British have a colony in Australia called New South Wales. Governor Darling has asked me to find waterways to cross this vast land.

Last night, my six men and I camped on a bank of the Murray River. This morning, as I wake up, Macleay, one of my men, says, "Mr. Sturt, our visitors have gone."

His news disappoints me. Several days ago, a large group of Aborigines befriended our party. Since then, four of them have travelled with us. *"Too bad!"* I say to Macleay. "I had hoped that they'd give us a friendly introduction to the next group."

After eating breakfast, we hoist the sail of our small whaleboat and continue on our voyage. A whaleboat is perfect for our explorations: it's roomy, about 25 feet long, has a sail, and can be taken apart and carried over land.

About ten miles into our trip, we see hundreds of armed and shouting Aborigines on a riverbank. Some have marked their bodies with white paint, making them look like skeletons; others have smeared themselves with red and yellow ochre. A lot of them are carrying darts and look like they've had a bucket of whitewash poured over their heads.

"Shall we avoid them?" Macleay asks.

"No," I tell him. "Our four Aboriginal friends are sure to be with them."

But when we get closer, the Aborigines increase their hostility, and I realize my mistake. *"Drop the sail and steer towards the center of the river!"* I shout to my men.

But my plan fails. A large number of Aborigines are running ahead to a sandbank jutting one-third of the way across the river. Standing up, I make signs to the Aborigines to go away, but they ignore me.

With a heavy heart, I take up my gun and say to my men, "Don't shoot until after I've fired both my barrels. I hope the fall of one man will save the lives of many."

As I put my finger on the trigger, Macleay shouts, *"Mr. Sturt, there are some other Aborigines on the other bank!"*

Turning, I see four Aborigines running at top speed. The leader throws himself into the river and swims to the sandbank. When he reaches it, he grabs the nearest hostile Aborigine by the throat and pushes him backwards. Then he walks furiously along the riverbank, points at our boat, shakes his fist, and stamps his feet on the sand.

My men and I watch overwhelmed with astonishment, and in truth stunned and confused; so singular, so unexpected, and so strikingly providential has been our escape.

Suddenly, our boat strikes ground, and we're startled into action. Looking around, I see a new stream joining the river. On one of the banks, there's a small group of Aborigines who are not armed.

Macleay turns to me and says, "Mr. Sturt, what should we do?"

TWO CHOICES FACE US: We can go to the aid of our Aboriginal friend, or we can land our boat on the bank of the new stream so that we'll be in a better position for a fight.

What should we do?

Answer:

I told my men to land the boat on the bank of the new stream where the group of unarmed Aborigines were standing.

When the hostile Aborigines saw us land, curiosity took the place of anger. All arguing stopped, and they swam over to us.

In less than a quarter of an hour from the moment we thought bloodshed unavoidable, we found ourselves peacefully surrounded by the hundreds who had so recently threatened us with destruction.

4 Edward Eyre: Murder in the Desert

What would you do if you were an explorer, and two of your guides murdered your companion?

The year is 1841. My name's Edward Eyre. I'm a 26-year-old British explorer. These days, the British are setting up colonies in Australia, and they need explorers to map out this vast land.

Two months ago, I set out on an expedition that will make me famous: a 1000-mile trip across southern Australia, from Fowler's Bay in South Australia to Albany in the west. Many colonists want a land route mapped out to move cattle from east to west, but I don't think such a route is possible because there's too much desert in southern Australia.

To help me on my difficult trip, I hired John Baxter, a British man who's a very good worker, and three Aboriginal guides: there's Wylie, who's from an Albany tribe, and two younger men from a different tribe. We brought eleven horses and six sheep with us.

Tonight, as we set up camp, I let out a harsh breath. The past two months have been awful. We've had to cross endless sand hills, getting sand in our clothes, hair, eyes, ears, food, and blankets, and the lack of water is a constant nightmare. If it weren't for my knowledgeable Aboriginal guides, I'd be dead. Who would have thought that the long roots of a single gum tree could give two-thirds of a pint of water?

Now winter is upon us, and the nights are bitterly cold. Also, our food rations are running low. The two younger guides want to turn back, but I'm determined to go on. So far, we've covered 400 miles of our 1000-mile trip.

Tonight, I'm on the first shift of the night watch. I have to follow the horses and sheep as they search for food.

"I'll see you at eleven," I call out to Baxter. He has the second shift.

The night passes slowly. But finally, at 10:30, I head back to camp. All of a sudden, I see a flare of light and hear a gunshot. I run towards the camp.

Wylie meets me. *"Come! Come!"* he cries.

He leads me to Baxter. Baxter is on the ground. He's been shot, and he's dying.

Looking around, I don't see the other two guides.. The camp is a mess and most of the food, water, and the guns are gone. *Good grief!* The other guides must have taken off with our supplies! Baxter must have surprised them, and they shot him. *Was Wylie involved?*

Suddenly, I'm filled with terror. Here I am in a wild and difficult land with a fierce wind raging, and the only company I have is a dying friend and a guide whose loyalty I'm unsure of. Even now, Wylie may be thinking of killing me. Of course, he could be entirely innocent.

Facing me, Wiley says, "Mr. Eyre, I had no idea what the others were up to. I was asleep when the gun went off. When I saw Mr. Baxter on the ground, I ran to meet you." He shakes his head. "All I know is that the boys asked me some time ago to go off with them."

Wiley and I spend an uneasy night. When the sun comes up, I wrap Baxter's body in a blanket: it would be impossible to bury him in this rocky, sandy land. After fixing a broken gun that the guides left behind, I decide to move on.

TWO CHOICES FACE ME: I can trust Wylie to continue on the journey with me, or I can send him away.

What should I do?

Answer:

I continued the trip with Wylie.

The two murderous guides followed us. I yelled at them to return to Fowler's Bay. I didn't want to shoot them. But they persisted.

"We don't want you. We want Wylie," they shouted.

When Wylie ignored them, they let out wild and mournful cries. After several days, they stopped following us.

Wylie and I had many more hardships on our journey, but as incredible as it seems we made it to Albany, a port city on the west coast of Australia. Our trip took over five months. Wylie's tribe was ecstatic to see him.

Although I was disappointed that I didn't find a good land route to move cattle, I was very happy to be alive. And just as I predicted, my name did go down in history: I was the first European to cross southern Australia by land from east to west.

5 Gonzalo Guerrero: Should I Go Back to My Old Life?

What would you do if you were captured by people in a strange land, and you had a chance to return to your old life after 8 years?

The year is 1519. My name's Gonzalo Guerrero. I'm a Spanish sailor. For the past 27 years, Spain has been trying to conquer lands in the areas you call Mexico and South America, as well as islands in the Caribbean. The Spanish king is greedy for gold and silver.

One day, eight years ago, while I was sailing near the coast of Mexico, my ship hit a rock. The ship was wrecked, but the crew and I made it to the shore. We were taken prisoner by a Mayan chief. Some of the crew were sacrificed to the Mayan gods and others died. Now, the only ones left are me and Geronimo de Aguilar. Geronimo is being kept in one village, while I'm living in another.

I look pretty different now: the Mayans tattooed my face, put holes in my ears, and slit my lower lip, just like they do for themselves. But my life is good. The chief gave me one of his daughters to marry and made me a chief.

This afternoon, as I'm talking to my wife, Geronimo walks into our village. *"Gonzalo!"* he cries. "A miracle has happened. Some of our countrymen have arrived in Mexico in ships. Their leader is Hernando Cortes. Cortes has sent messengers with gifts to buy our freedom." Geronimo is breathless with excitement. "Can you believe it, Gonzalo? You and I can leave this place and return to Spain!"

Geronimo's news seems incredible. A long time ago, I gave up the hope of being rescued.

TWO CHOICES FACE ME: I can return to my old life in Spain, or I can stay in Mexico.

What should I do?

Answer:

I looked at my friend and said, "Geronimo, I'm going to stay here. Just imagine what the Spaniards would say if they saw me in such a state, with my face tattooed, my ears bored, and my lip split? Anyhow, I have three sons, and look what handsome boys they are."

Geronimo gave me a shocked look and said, "Gonzalo, don't be foolish. Remember that you're a good Christian, and your Mayan wife is not a Christian. Anyhow, if you love your wife and sons, take them with you."

But I was firm and said, "No, Geronimo, my mind is made up. I'm going to stay here."

Point of Interest:

Gonzalo Guerrero was worried about what the Spaniards would think of him when they saw his tattoos, ear piercings, and lip piercing. Would he have to worry today?

6   Hernando Cortes: We Must Be Dreaming

What would you do if you had conquered an empire, and the people rebelled?

The year is 1519. My name's Hernando Cortes. I'm a Spanish soldier of fortune. I want to conquer kingdoms so that I can get rich.

Seven months ago, I landed in Mexico, home of the Aztec Empire, which has lots of gold and silver. With 600 men, I began marching towards the Aztec capital, Tenochtitlan, which you call Mexico City.

Already Montezuma, the Aztec Emperor, has sent messengers to see me and has sent me amazing gifts made of gold and silver. He must be very rich.

My goal is to take over Montezuma's great kingdom. Although he rules millions of people, I think I can conquer him because the people he rules are from different tribes, and many are unhappy. *"Montezuma is cruel!"* they say. "He uses our people for sacrifices to the gods and he taxes us heavily." Some want to help me fight Montezuma. In fact, about 6000 of them are marching with me towards the great capital.

Today, my men and I are finally going to make it to Mexico City. As we approach the imperial city, several hundred Aztec nobles welcome us, dressed in their finest clothes. One by one they greet me, which takes a lot of time. And all the while, we're surrounded by many people who are curious to see us.

As we ride our horses towards the city, Diaz, the soldier riding next to me, cries, *"Good heavens! I must be dreaming! I've never seen a city so beautiful!"*

The marvelous Aztec capital is built on an island in a lake. There are two volcanoes in the background, and amazing stone towers, pyramids, and buildings rise above turquoise water. The island is joined to the mainland by three causeways. Montezuma's imperial city looks like something out of a fairy tale.

As we enter the city, there are people everywhere. Montezuma approaches on a royal litter, completely surrounded by nobles. In the front of his procession, three officials are carrying golden wands. When Montezuma gets closer, I see that his litter is being carried on the shoulders of nobles who are barefoot.

Montezuma gets off the litter and walks towards me, looking every inch a great emperor. He's wearing a fancy cape, arm and leg decorations, colorful bird feathers, and sandals made with many jewels and soles of gold. As Montezuma walks, nobles sweep the ground before him and put down cloths for him to walk on. They also shelter him from the sun with a bright green canopy made of feathers, gold, silver, pearls, and jewels.

I jump off my horse and walk towards Montezuma, studying him carefully. The great chief looks to be about 40 years old. He has an athletic build, a small beard, and a face that is long and merry. We salute one another, and I step forward and place a colored glass necklace around his neck.

Using a translator, Montezuma says, "My Lord, I've prepared a palace for you to stay. Cuitlahuac, my brother, will escort you."

As we walk along, we pass a market with thousands of people. *"Good grief!"* Diaz says. "The people are selling everything: bricks, hairless dogs, chili peppers, frogs, insect eggs, medicines, love potions, and make-up." He laughs. "I can't believe it. The customers are paying with cocoa beans!" When we reach our accommodation, we're amazed. Incredibly, Montezuma has given me and my men one of his royal palaces to stay in.

During the days that follow, Montezuma treats us like royalty.

One night, a few of my men come to see me. "Captain Cortes," they say. "None of us can sleep. There are only a few hundred of us and a hundred thousand Aztecs in this city. We're afraid that we may be killed at any moment."

I nod and say, "I'm worried too, but I have a plan. I think we should protect ourselves by taking Montezuma hostage." My men agree to my plan.

To our great surprise, Montezuma lets us take him prisoner without a fuss.

For six months, we keep Montezuma hostage, and things go well. Even though he is a prisoner, Montezuma is in good spirits: he jokes with us and teaches us games to play.

But now, I'm in trouble. Not long ago, I had to leave the city for a few weeks. I left one of my men in charge, and he behaved very badly: he attacked a large group of Aztecs who were at a feast and butchered many of them. Now, the Aztecs are rebelling.

Desperate, I go to see Montezuma. "Montezuma," I say, "you must try to calm your people."

Montezuma agrees to help me and tries to calm his people, but they curse and throw stones at him. Shockingly, Montezuma is injured, and later he dies. The Aztecs turn murderous.

"We must escape," I tell my men. As quick as we can, we rush out of the city, but the Aztecs chase us. As we make our escape, we lose hundreds of men. Finally, we make it to safety.

TWO CHOICES FACE ME: I can leave Mexico, or I can organize another army to attack the Aztec capital.

What should I do?

Answer:

Over the next ten months, I built up another army, recruiting enemies of the Aztecs. We marched towards Mexico City. Once there, I cut off the Aztec's food supply.

My plan worked: after 93 days, I conquered the Aztec Empire.

Point of Interest:

There are several reasons why the Aztec Empire, with its millions of people, was conquered by a few hundred Spaniards:

-- the Spaniards carried diseases to Mexico that the First Peoples had no immunity against, like smallpox, typhus, measles, and influenza, and these diseases killed up to 90% of the First Peoples in some settlements;

-- Montezuma had many enemies who sided with Cortes;

-- and Cortes and his men had better weapons, like guns, crossbows, and cannons.

7 Alexander Selkirk: The Real Robinson Crusoe

What would you do if you were stranded on an island, and unfriendly sailors landed on your shores?

The year is 1704. My name's Alexander Selkirk. I'm the son of a Scottish shoemaker. Wanting adventure, I joined a band of buccaneers; they're pirates secretly approved by the English king to steal from his enemies.

Two years ago, after an argument with my captain, I was abandoned on an uninhabited island in the South Pacific Ocean, 400 miles from the coast of Chile. This island is called Juan Fernandez.

For months, I had to bear up against deep sadness and the terror of being left alone in such an isolated place; but the many jobs I had to do in order to survive helped me to get over my fear of being alone. There were huts to build, wild goats to hunt, lobsters and fish to catch, and turnips, cabbage-palms and parsnips to harvest.

There are lots of cats on the island, so I tamed some kittens. I wanted them to stop the rats from chewing on my feet and clothes at night. The cats, rats, and goats came ashore from previous ships.

To amuse myself, I read, pray, sing, and dance with my tame goats and cats. Although I'm used to my life, there's nothing I'd like more than to return to civilization.

Today, as I walk along the beach, I get a shock. A ship is anchored nearby. When I see that it's a Spanish ship, I become uneasy. "Well, cats," I say, "what shall I do? It's a Spanish ship. If it were a French ship, I'd immediately try to attract the sailors' attention, but the Spaniards don't like foreign sailors. Too many have stolen the gold they're shipping from South America to Spain. If they find me, they'll probably take me as a slave or kill me."

Suddenly, I see Spanish sailors walking in my direction. When they see me, they stop walking. In silence, we stare at one another.

TWO CHOICES FACE ME: I can try to befriend the sailors, or I can run away.

What should I do?

Answer:

I ran away. As soon as I did, the Spaniards shot at me and chased me into the woods. Since I was very fit from having hunted wild goats, I was too fast for them. When I was out of sight, I climbed a tree. It was pretty terrifying when some of the sailors came very near to kill goats. They had only to look up to see me. But they didn't. When the Spaniards sailed away, I climbed down the tree and returned to my solitary life. I was overjoyed to see the sails of their ship disappear into the distance.

Points of Interest:

Two years after this incident, British sailors in two ships, the Duchess and the Duke, rescued me when I made a fire to get their attention. The sailors were shocked at the sight of me: an odd figure of a man clothed in goat-skins from head to foot, with a long beard, shaggy hair, and a face tanned black. Woodes Rogers, the captain of the Duke, described me as "a Man cloth'd in Goat-Skins, who look'd wilder than the first Owners of them." After four years of being alone, I was almost incoherent with joy.

On their arrival, many of the English sailors were sick with scurvy, so I made them good food to eat like boiled cabbage. In no time their scurvy was cured and they were healthy again. Eventually, I made it back to England. [NB: Scurvy is caused by a vitamin C deficiency. Cabbage contains vitamin C.]

I was the inspiration for the novel Robinson Crusoe.

What is the first thing you would miss if you were stranded on a small island?

8 Father Lacombe: *Nothing to Eat!*

What would you do if you didn't have enough food for yourself, and you met some starving people?

It is the winter of 1867. My name's Father Lacombe. I'm a Catholic priest. I preach in the area you call the Canadian prairies, teaching the word of God to wandering First Peoples. While visiting their camps, I've become a friend of the Cree, Blackfoot, and Sarcee.

This winter, I'm on a mission to visit many camps of First Peoples. I have two companions travelling with me: Alexis, my guide, and Suzanne, an elderly Blackfoot woman who's teaching me her language.

So far, the weather has been brutally cold, and we've seen a lot of misery. For weeks, we have been tending to the sick and the hungry, and this has nearly exhausted our food supply. Two days ago, we left for another Cree camp.

This afternoon, as we trudge along, Alexis turns to me and says, "Father, the snow is very deep. We'd better stop here for the night."

Suddenly we see smoke coming from a clump of trees. "That must be a camp," I say to Alexis. "Let's make ourselves known."

At the camp, we find two Cree families huddled together in a teepee. There are eighteen people altogether. *"Good heavens!"* I cry. "These people are nothing but skin and bones. The children are too weak to cry." I crouch before one of the Cree men. "What happened?" I ask.

In a low voice, he says, "We came down from the forest country. There was no good hunting there, and we had to eat our dogs and horses. We decided to travel south to look for our relatives and to hunt for buffalo, but now we are too weak to continue."

TWO CHOICES FACE ME: I can feed the starving Cree and risk the lives of my own little group, or I can keep my small amount of food and try to find help for the Cree.

What should I do?

Answer:

I turned to Alexis and Suzanne and said, "I would like to feed these people our remaining six frozen fish and the bit of meat we have left." Alexis agreed, and so did Suzanne, saying, "I've often starved before, Father."

After eating our food, the Cree gained enough strength to join us on our journey. The next day, Alexis caught a rabbit and a partridge. We cooked the meat and gave it to the children.

It took a huge effort to drag ourselves across the prairie. After five days of hiking, we reached our destination but were greatly disappointed: the Cree camp had moved.

The next day, I got weaker. At times, my mind went blank and my vision blurred. To survive, we made soup from water and old hide sacks and straps. Alexis managed to get a few pieces of buffalo meat from a scabby, sick, and dying buffalo that he killed, but the meat looked and smelled awful. The Cree eagerly ate it. I ate some too, but vomited right way. I said to Alexis, "We'll have to do something soon. More than two weeks have passed since we ate a proper meal. If we don't find the camp tomorrow, we'll have to kill a horse."

Early the following day, we set off on our trek again. To our great joy, we spotted the Cree camp. *We'd made it!* Lucky for us, the Cree had plenty of buffalo meat to share. But because we were so weak, the Cree only fed us broth containing little pieces of chopped buffalo for the first couple of days so that we wouldn't make ourselves sick. Then we ate as much as we wanted.

My ordeal of nearly starving to death taught me a valuable lesson. I wrote a letter to friends telling them about my experiences, saying, *"...how painful and torturing it is to know hunger in circumstances like these!"*

I told my friends that I was wrong to have preached that people who did not want to work should not eat, saying, "But now, after such an experience, I have changed my ideas, and I have taken the resolution to share my last mouthful with anyone who is hungry. After experiencing such hardship from hunger, how clearly one understands these words of the Father of the poor: 'I was hungry, and you gave Me nothing to eat.'"

NB: The quote "I was hungry, and you gave Me nothing to eat." comes from the Bible, Matthew 25:42, in which Jesus chastises people who refuse to feed those who are hungry.

9 Manuela Saenz: Enemies at the Door

What would you do if you were staying with a freedom fighter, and his enemies showed up at the door?

The year is 1828. My name's Manuela Saenz. At present, I'm in Bogota, in the country you call Colombia. My life is in danger because I'm helping the freedom fighter Simon Bolivar. Already, Bolivar has freed many parts of South America from Spain. You call these areas Venezuela, Colombia, Ecuador, Peru, and Bolivia.

For 300 years, the Spanish have exploited the South American people and taken their riches, ever since they conquered the Inca.

Bolivar's heroic actions have earned him the nickname *The Liberator*. But at present, there's a lot of danger in the streets as different political factions fight Bolivar for control of the government.

On this night, Bolivar and I are in an apartment in the government palace. Suddenly, I hear a strange noise. *"Bolivar,"* I whisper, *"I think we're in danger."*

The Liberator immediately takes up his sword and pistol and goes to the door. From the corridor, we hear people shout, *"Death to the tyrant!"*

I say to Bolivar, "Don't open the door!" Then I rush to a window. "This would be a good window to jump from!" I tell him.

Bolivar crosses the room and opens the window. Looking outside, I make sure the coast is clear; then Bolivar jumps out the window.

Seconds later, the door to our room bursts open and rebels barge in. Desperate to give Bolivar some time to escape, I rush towards the rebels in an effort to distract them. Too bad I didn't have time to shut the window.

Grabbing me, they shout, *"Where's Bolivar?"*

TWO CHOICES FACE ME: I can lie to the rebels to give Bolivar a few precious moments to escape, which could get me killed, or I can tell the truth, which could get Bolivar killed.

What should I do?

Answer:

I lied to the rebels. "Bolivar is in the council chamber," I told them.

They pointed to the open window. *"He has escaped!"* they cried.

I shook my head. "No, gentlemen. He has not escaped. He's in the council room."

"Then why is this window open?" they asked.

I shrugged and said, "I opened it to see what the noise was."

After a thorough search, the rebels knew that I'd lied. They gave me a severe beating, but I didn't care. Bolivar had escaped. To keep safe, he had hidden under a bridge until he learned that the rebels had been defeated. Their assassination attempt had failed. This was the second time that Bolivar's enemies had tried to assassinate him.

Points of Interest:

Bolivar continued fighting to free South America from Spanish rule, but he didn't have much longer to live: he died of tuberculosis two years after this incident. He was 47. Many South Americans consider Bolivar a hero. Bolivia was named after him.

10 Irena Sendlerowa: Should I Become a Secret Agent?

What would you do if it were wartime, and you could save the lives of many children if you became a secret agent?

The year is 1942. My name's Irena Sendlerowa. I'm a 32-year-old social worker. I live in Warsaw, Poland.

These are terrible times. Atrocities are happening every day. World War II is raging, and the Germans have taken over much of Poland.

The Nazis rule Germany, and they don't like Jewish people. They've built a brick wall ten feet high and eleven miles long around the neighborhoods in Warsaw where many Jewish people live. This area is called the Warsaw Ghetto. The Nazis are forcing 400,000 Jewish people to live inside the Ghetto, and they don't let them out. Conditions in the Ghetto are terrible. Many Jews are dying from starvation and disease.

In a surprising move, the Germans are now offering to send many unhappy Jewish citizens to special holiday camps, but I know what's really happening: the Germans are sending them to concentration camps where they'll be killed. They're even killing the children.

Today, as I walk around the Ghetto, I'm horrified at the thought of what will happen to all these beautiful people. "Well, Irena," I think to myself, "what are you going to do? Because you work for the health department, you have permission to go into the Ghetto, which puts you in a good position to help."

I sit down on a crate and look at some children playing. Maybe I could become an agent in the secret organization Zegota. Zegota rescues Jewish people in German-held territory.

Looking at the brick wall surrounding the Ghetto, I realize the danger of my idea. Being a secret agent would be dangerous. If I get caught, the Germans will surely kill me.

TWO CHOICES FACE ME: I can become a secret agent, or I can do nothing as our Jewish citizens are being murdered.

What should I do?

Answer:

I joined Zegota and organized a small group of social workers to smuggle Jewish children out of the Ghetto to safety. We hid them in ambulances, took them through sewers, wheeled them out in suitcases or boxes, and smuggled them out through a courtyard that led to non-Jewish areas. We changed the children's names and placed them with Polish families.

In total, we saved 2500 children. Because I wanted them to be reunited with their families in the future, I wrote their names on cigarette papers, put the papers in glass bottles, and buried the bottles in a garden. When World War II was over, the lists were given to Jewish representatives and attempts were made to reunite the children with their families, but most family members had died in concentration camps.

In 1943, I was arrested, taken to Nazi headquarters, and badly beaten. My legs and feet were broken. The Germans drove me away to be killed, but a sack full of dollars paid by Zegota got me freed. The Germans dumped me by the roadside. For the rest of my life, I had to use crutches.

Point of Interest:

In 2007, sixty-two years after World War II ended, the Polish parliament honored me as a national hero, and I was nominated for the Nobel peace prize. I was 97 years old. Journalists visited me in the nursing home where I lived.

"How does it feel to be a hero?" they asked.

"I didn't do anything special," I told them. "I was brought up to believe that a person must be rescued when drowning, no matter what their religion or nationality. It annoys me very much to be called a hero. I don't feel like a hero. The opposite is true: my conscience still bothers me because I feel I did so little."

* * * * *

Free Sample: "What Country Am I?" Geography Series

Fish Skin Jackets?

What country would you be in if you were having a business meeting in a sauna?

Here are some more hints.

1. I'm in northern Europe.

2. I'm the birthplace of the sauna. Many people have a sauna in their home and in their cottage. If you come to my country to do a business deal, don't be surprised if the company boss tells you that the meeting will take place in the company sauna.

Here's a lesson in sauna procedure: sit in a small room and sweat it out by pouring water over heated rocks. Do this until you feel faint. Then cool down in a cold shower; or if you're really brave, roll around in the snow or jump in an icy lake. I know it sounds painful, but it's actually very refreshing.

3. My winters are very cold. That's because I'm as far north as Iceland, Alaska, and Siberia. One third of my land is above the Arctic Circle, where there is continuous daylight for several weeks in summer and continuous darkness for several weeks in winter. It's like having one really long day, and one really long night. Some people find my long, dark winters very depressing. Maybe that's why my people are the biggest coffee drinkers in the world.

4. Mosquitoes are so bad in my country that my people hold a World Mosquito-Killing Championship each summer. The prize goes to the person who kills the most mosquitoes in a given amount of time using only the hands. One record was for 21 mosquitos killed in five minutes. But be warned: my people are very good because they get so much practice.

5. My people have names like Eeva-Liisa Manner, Lasse Hallstrom, and Paavo Saarinen.

6. The name of my country means "land of the Finns". Finn comes from the Germanic word finna, which means fish scale. In early times, Finns wore clothes made of many different kinds of skins, including fish skins. Maybe that's how they got their name.

What country am I?

Answer: Finland.

Points of Interest:

If you visit me, you can go on a snow safari in Lapland province in the north. It lies mostly above the Arctic Circle and has snow ten months of the year. Lapland is huge and flat, and some areas have hardly any people. The Sami have lived in Lapland for thousands of years, and some still herd reindeer.

For fun, you can hire a guide to take you on a reindeer sled or a dog sled. Then you can set out across one of the many frozen lakes and take a journey into nowhere. But don't be surprised if your guide's cell phone rings. My people are cell phone crazy! This is hardly surprising since Nokia, which makes cell phones, has its roots in my country.

It's not what you do in life; it's how you do it.

TITLES BY MC PAQUIN

Fiction Book

Fen Parker: Wormhole Chronicles
Reluctant Time Traveler

What Should I Do? Series

The Sphinx & the Pharaoh

Cleopatra's Carpet Trick

Michelangelo's Problem Apprentice

Saved by the Tail of an Ox

The King's Poison Bread

The Hand of Peace; The Hand of War

Lost, Starving, and Naked in the New World

The Real Robinson Crusoe

Lincoln in Love

What Country Am I? Series

Possums in the Attic

A Beauty Contest for Men

Look a Gorilla in the Eye

Very Short Picture History Books

Yay! A Short Picture History of Canada in 60 Minutes!

Yay! A Short Picture History of the USA in 60 Minutes!

Printed in Great Britain
by Amazon